SURVIVING
SUCCESSION

SURVIVING
SUCCESSION

A Small Business Owner's Guide to Moving On

ALEX TEECE

CONTENTS

INTRODUCTION

Imagine, for a moment, that time has stopped, and you get to step back and look at the years - decades, even - that you have spent founding, owning, managing, and leading a business. At this point, you have worked so hard that time seems to have just passed you by. You lost yourself in your company, in your projects and deals, in your passion to grow and provide. You provided for employees and families - maybe even competitors. You showed up early, left late, and people looked to you as the backbone, the cornerstone to the business you had become synonymous with – you and your business were one. You worked so hard that you never once considered your leadership transition, a transfer of ownership, or a succession plan.

And then, one day, you woke up and thought: *I think I'd like to do something else now.* It's like that scene from Forrest Gump when, after Forrest has spent years running across the country, he suddenly stops one day and says, "I'm pretty tired – I think I'll go home now." Something in you changed or shifted. It wasn't overnight, and perhaps you had glimpses of it along the way, over the years. But now, the spark that ignited you each day to go to your business and own, manage, and lead is replaced with a wondering: *what's next for me?*

This book is a short, straightforward, easy-to-digest series of topics and questions to help you not only explore the answer to this wondering, but to begin taking small, meaningful steps toward the rest of your life. *Surviving Succession* is just that, surviving the challenging, grueling series of hurdles that, if left unplanned for and unchecked, will take your business down, and likely you down with it.

90% of family businesses just like yours do not last past three generations, and nearly 9 in 10 entrepreneur-founded small companies eventually fail – this is not coincidence. And while you are unique, you are not unlike the tens of thousands of business owners who, like you, have gone to work every day for the past 10, 20, or even 30 years and thought at one point recently, "I can't do this forever, and maybe it's time to think about what's next, and how my business will fare without me."

The answer to this wondering lies in two places: one, in part, is this book; and two, more importantly, it lies within you – but, only if you prompt the reflections, planning, and processes necessary to begin your journey away from your business and towards the life you will live afterward. This life, which is waiting for you, is one of new beginnings, new memories, and a rested, refreshed you.

I have written, led, studied, and advised on countless succession plans over the past decade. I wrote and executed my own following COVID and supported a board, leadership team, employees, and clients in not only accepting the reality, but also living its benefits. There is a reason we call it "surviving" – you truly have to continue to exist as an individual, separate from your business, and endure despite the difficult circumstances and challenges that may be in your path.

This book covers those challenges, the life on the other side of them, and how to get there. Think of it as a short, three-part survival kit that clearly and succinctly paints a picture of the wilderness setting in around you, the safe and open field you are trying to get to, and the path to get there. The path is narrow, treacherous, and full of twists and turns back into the thicket – but there does exist a path, and to get to that safe and open field, you need to find this path, follow it, and trust that it will lead you where you truly want to be.

Where you want to be is where so many others just like you, who have lived a life of business ownership and service to employees, customers, and family want to be. It is a life where your business legacy has been written, and the chapter of your ownership and management has been appreciated, honored, and closed. It is a life of bucket lists, grandchildren, hobbies, and leisure. You have earned it, and it is waiting for you.

If you are not planning on working forever, and you are not entirely sure how to leave, this book is for you. It will serve as a compass. And while a compass alone will not get you to your destination, it will orient you through the journey ahead. If used correctly, it will ensure you survive.

That is the goal: survival. *Surviving Succession* may not be the only thing you need to help you move on from your business, but it will surely help prepare you and make sense of the journey ahead.

Let's begin.

PART 1

The Serious Risk You Face Without A Succession Strategy

CHAPTER 1

Do You Know How to Get Out?

"I'm here for one reason and one reason alone. I'm here to guess what the music might do a week, a month, a year from now. That's it. Nothing more. And standing here tonight, I'm afraid that I don't hear a thing. Just... silence."

- John Tuld, Margin Call

Do you know when the music will stop?

Imagine. You are sitting on a beach, or at your granddaughter's softball game, or in a river fly fishing. Someone approaches you and asks, *"How did you ever leave the business you founded? What did you do to get out?"* What do you tell them?

Picture yourself, 30 years ago, as a young, visionary entrepreneur: a leader. You began building a business, a team, a group of clients. You grew day by day, and over the course of weeks, months, and years, you made your business into what it is today - you became who you are today. From the ground up, you created something.

Bootstraps, luck, whatever you want to call it - you made this. It is yours.

Along the way, you weren't looking into the distant future asking yourself: when will be my last day? Who will take over for me? What will become of this when I leave? You were too busy building; you were too busy living.

And yet, in the coming years, millions of baby boomers will enter a well-deserved retirement and transition into a life of hobbies, travel, grandparenting, and solace. The U.S. Census estimates that there are approximately 71 million people in the country who were born between 1946 and 1964.[1] Recent surveys estimate that family firms comprise 80-90% of all businesses in the U.S., contributing more than 60% of GDP and over 77% of all jobs.[2] There are tens of thousands of small business owners who have started, owned, and grown businesses for decades, working their way through recessions, crises, pandemics, and a technological revolution. Tens of thousands of people who have stories similar to yours. Tens of thousands who have questions that are unanswered, who are unsure how to proceed now that they are nearing the end of their business entrepreneurship, leadership, and ownership road.

And now, you are no longer in the Wild West days of business building and bootstrapping, leaning into the unknown of entrepreneurial wonder and creating your company as you go. Your focus is now on your legacy and on the future. Like you, there are many who will navigate a similar path in the years ahead. The

---

[1] 2020 Census Will Help Policymakers Prepare for the Incoming Wave of Aging Boomers, December 2019

[2] More than 8 out of 10 family businesses have no succession plans, Boston Globe, 2016

problem - where is that path, how do you follow it, and how do you know where it leads?

Where is your "get out" plan?

More likely than not, you do not have a succession plan in place. The fact is, most family businesses, small and medium in size, do not have an exit strategy for their founder that includes clear, methodical, strategic structures and procedures in place to ensure a smooth transition for self, business, and family. In 2022, the Royal Bank of Canada reported that 61% of family-owned businesses did not have a succession plan in place.[3] More likely than not, this number will only increase as more and more family business founders and owners head into the age of retirement and face down their final days as leaders of their companies.

Yet, as a business owner and leader, the moment will come, as it has so many times before, when your employees, clients, and family members will look to you and ask, "What's next?" At that moment, what will your answer be? How will you reassure them that in your absence, the company - and the family - may actually be better off?

A true succession plan takes years to build, as it involves the development of people and processes to slowly and strategically remove you from the center of the company.

Imagine being in an operating room and watching a doctor who is performing a critical procedure in a life-saving surgery - they

---

[3] Succession-planning tips for family businesses, Royal Bank of Canada, 2024

have practiced, trained, and communicated with their team and the nurses who will be responsible for the patient once surgery is done. The smooth, choreographed handoff is part of a continuum of care.

Or imagine an Olympic athlete who trains, studies, and perfects that moment of exchange during a relay race. They know how fast, at which point in their stride, and how close to be to their teammate when they hand off the baton. This moment of critical importance does not come and go without diligence, planning, and preparation.

So why do a majority of small business owners not only have no plan in place, but also have not developed a bench of capable leaders, a company resilient to managerial change, and a client base who will not flinch in this stage of transition? These are the questions we seek to ask, and answer, over the next several chapters as you piece together the tenets of a strong, working, go-forward succession strategy.

Business and leadership transition is as much of an art as it is a science, but the science must be methodical and intentional. Your company depends on you, your family depends on you, and a working plan can and will make all the difference as you transition away from decades of being the boss to a new life of possibility for yourself, your loved ones, and your future.

How much time do you actually have?

Not to sound morbid, but this question is on the minds of many retiring business leaders. At the intersection of your business and personal life is the most precious and finite resource that you have – time. Your time is the input and the driver in all of the decisions you make - not only within the business you have built but within the life you live. It is fleeting, it is limited, and you will never get it back. Ever.

Consider your current allocation of time between your business and personal life - is it 50/50? 75/25? 90/10? What if you divide it between your present actions vs. preparing for your future – do you spend any time at all strategizing for the future?

Did you know that nearly 9 out of 10 leadership teams spend less than one hour per month discussing strategy? 50% spend no time at all.[4] Imagine that - literally every other leader doesn't plan for the future of their business. This critical intersection of direction and purpose provides a moment of tension regarding the decision that you have to make around your business, succession plan, and exit strategy.

The moment of tension is this - if I stay, just a little longer, what improved economic value can I bring to my business, my family, and myself? Is there another big contract right around the corner? Or a deal that is almost closed? Your willingness to never give up has brought you success, and in a way, exiting your business can feel like "giving up" on what you've built.

---

[4] The Office of Strategy Management, 2005

But you are not giving up. You are giving way to the next wave of energy, perspective, and leadership that will take your company forward. You are tying up loose ends of the past so you can focus on the future. You are leaning away from your responsibilities as president and CEO and towards a refreshed identity of yourself. This moment of questioning "worth" from a personal and business sense is challenging, albeit common, with founders who are heading towards the finish line of their business and the starting line of the rest of their life.

As cliché as it may sound, the one thing we cannot get back is time. The longer we maintain the image of ourselves as business people and leaders, the longer we delay the inevitable, which is that our legacy is waiting for us and cannot truly begin until we have passed the torch and moved on. The value of our business may come down to a number on a piece of paper, but the value of our time cannot, and will not, ever be measured until we and others look back at how much we had and what we did with it.

You are not getting any younger. Your legacy is waiting, and time is ticking.

CHAPTER 2

Problems On The Horizon and Beyond

"Fredo, you're my older brother, and I love you. But don't ever take sides with anyone against the Family again. Ever"

- Michael Corleone, The Godfather

Building a business over the course of your life has likely been a challenging and deeply personal feat that has shaped who you are today. It's no wonder that you would not want to hand it off to just anyone as you step back from ownership and into the next chapter of your life. But, if you are similar to so many business founders out there, you likely have not spent your life cultivating the next crop of managers and leaders, bringing family - successfully - into the fray, and planning a smooth exit into your business afterlife. This could come back to haunt you now as you realize: *I don't want to work forever, and I don't know who will help me leave the way I want to.* Who can you trust?

You have no bench of leaders to take your place

NBA players are developed in college and the G League; hockey stars in 'Juniors;' baseball players in farm leagues. Years of practice, coaching, and training lead to their moment on the biggest and brightest of stages. And yet, when it comes to business, there is no farm league or developmental team required; no factory of young stars. Do you have a development program for future leaders of your company? Do you trust the people who are in line to take over your life's work?

Building a deep bench of future successors, especially while you are working to survive the day-to-day of growing and leading your own company, is a tall order for anyone. Yet it is critical to the success of a business to find, nurture, and grow people internally to ensure there will be multiple candidates ready for the role.[5] This process must take place months, if not years, in advance of succession if you want to ensure the company will move forward and survive.

So, who is on your bench? For many owners, handing down the family business to the next generation is the fairytale ending to a life spent building a company. Other owners opt to choose non-family successors, who may be key employees or external players in the industry. Once you know who you want on your bench, your task is to set these people up for success in the months and years before your exit.

---

[5] CEO succession starts with developing your leaders, McKinsey & Co., 2015

Yet many owners approaching their exit have no bench of people to succeed them. They do not have an internal group of candidates, an external pipeline of potential leaders, or an advisory board to ensure a regular, healthy cadence of preparation. They do not have a developmental strategy for candidate readiness, a transition plan, or any managerial structure to ensure robust cross-training and exposure.

The results of the above scenario – a company that will immediately and absolutely become hesitant, unsure, and leaderless without its founder and owner, like a flinch. A company that, historically and statistically speaking, is bound for failure and begins to bleed clients and succumb to the pressures of everyday operation - pressures that for a long time were managed, effectively and adequately, by you. Now, no one is in charge, and the impact can be catastrophic.

With no bench of leaders, you are banking on the remaining people to somehow, against all odds, figure it out. You are counting on chance. Are you willing to bet your company and your legacy on this?

Family challenges

Mario Puzo's *The Godfather* offers us many memorable one-liners and moments, perhaps none greater than the exchange between Michael Corleone and his brother Fredo. Following his support of Mo Green, Fredo turns to his younger brother, Michael, and chastises him for his approach to doing business with Mo in Las Vegas. Michael turns to him and says, "Fredo, you're my older brother, and I love you. But don't ever take sides with anyone against the Family again. Ever."

While we are likely not living the lives of Mafia brothers, this moment reminds us of the importance of familial alignment in business, deference, and perhaps most importantly - loyalty. With no bench of leaders, and conflicting family and family-like relationships within and proximate to the business, family involvement with succession planning and execution often takes a negative turn towards siloed interests and a toxic operating culture. Look no further than the HBO show *Succession* to get a dramatized, and somewhat over-the-top, depiction of the events that can unfold once people get a taste of what might be theirs.

Perhaps this is why only 40% of family businesses are passed to second-generation owners (seemingly correlated with the lack of succession planning), only 12% are passed to third-generation owners, and perhaps most significantly, only 3% of businesses are passed to owners who are fourth generation and beyond. In short, after three generations, 97% of businesses have fallen into non-family hands.[6]

> *A different path – I was sitting in a coffee shop recently and overheard a conversation between a father and his son. The father was telling his son that he didn't know how many years he had left in the business, which was a bakery, not to mention in his life. He asked the son if he would consider taking over, and the son said, "I love you, Dad, but I am not a baker, and I have my own dreams – they are different*

---

6 Johnson College of Business, Cornell University, Family Business Facts, 2024

from yours." The father looked down at the table, and his son reached out and grabbed his father's hands. The father looked up, and through misty eyes, he nodded, offering, without words, his acceptance of his son's decision. Like so many other children of founders and owners, the son's vision for his career and his life was different. And like so many other founders, the father now had to accept that the generational handoff stopped with him. He was left to reckon with the succession legacy he did not have and find a way forward for his business, alone.

Family businesses can offer incredible longevity in terms of culture, service, and overall orientation of the organization. However, family changes, and as seen in *The Godfather* and countless other fictional examples (e.g., *Succession*), children and extended family have different views of success and varying degrees of loyalty. When not properly planned for, navigated, and managed, handing a business off to family quickly becomes complex and messy, sometimes altering family relationships beyond repair. A plan is imperative.

Family dynamics tend to come into focus once people realize what they stand to gain or lose, given a pending succession and change in leadership. If you do not get far ahead of these complexities, they will determine the path for you, as they have for so many.

An unclear and uncertain (business) afterlife

In the last chapter, we discussed time and pondered what your time is worth as a current business leader as opposed to a former business leader. The concept and allocation of one's time says a lot about what one values, what brings one joy, and where one will have the greatest impact on others, including employees, family, and people who have counted on them for so long.

Similarly, a challenge that many people experience in their after-business life is the feeling an artist must get when they see a blank canvas or that a musician must get when they see a sheet without music. "Where do I go from here? What do I bring with me? What do I leave behind?"

Reinventing oneself is an incredibly difficult, emotional, and perhaps spiritual journey that, at least for business leaders and people of consequence, is very, very difficult to achieve in earnest. There are layers and levels to this reinvention, with moments of stagnation and setbacks.

Reimagining and redefining one's identity against the backdrop of stepping away from relevance, responsibility, and power can be confusing for many former leaders. This happens more often than not when the allure of retirement and lack of responsibility eventually gives way to consternation and confusion, and a former CEO or president asks themselves: "What is my sense of purpose? Who am I now as a past leader of a business?"

You may not be able to answer these questions now, but you can begin to live into what an answer might be. Meaning, how can you move forward and begin this renaissance if you are stuck in the present, or even worse, the past? The consequences of these problems can be far-reaching and long-lasting if not dealt with. Often, they must be handled before and during the succession journey. If not, they are left to fester and wait for you as you step away from your business and into your life.

CHAPTER 3

The Fallout

"In any organization, there comes a time when the leader has to ask whether it's time for fresh energy."

- Howard Schultz

A business that suffers

Let's be clear: just because you leave, your business is not guaranteed to fail. In fact, it might flourish. If prepared, it likely will.

Did you know that two out of every three family-owned businesses fail or are sold?[7] A sale is not necessarily a mark of failure, but what if it was not on your terms? What if you sold your life's work for pennies on the dollar to *Barbarians at the Gate* (see "The Fall of RJR Nabisco")? Last chapter, we highlighted that only one in ten family businesses make it to a fourth generation. What happens along the way to chip away at the longevity and promise of a

---

[7] Avoid the Traps That Can Destroy Family Businesses, Harvard Business Review, 2012

family firm that can withstand generations of change? Why is it that nine out of ten do not last, are sold off, or fail?

What we do know is that there is often a "dip" when a founder leaves. A dip in clarity of direction, a dip in morale, and a dip in business. There is nothing worse than a bad succession - literally. It is estimated that up to 50% of new leaders fail in the first 18 months of their new role.[8] A major, contributing factor to this quick exit and increased turnover: the lack of deliberate, strategic, and supported succession planning and execution. The new leader does not know where to go, they have no momentum, and they feel lost. Employees and clients may be looking for you (you are gone), competitors are circling like sharks (blood in the water), and the company is sailing, rudderless, into the abyss. Your life's work and legacy are just drifting into irrelevance.

Without fully preparing your successor for - and letting go of - the responsibilities that come with executive leadership, your company will be stifled in the moments leading up to and through succession, left hobbled by a leader who is unable to effectively hand over the reins.

> *The uncomfortable Thanksgiving dinner – I had a client who was in business with his father repairing older, European cars. The father had inherited the business from his own father and taught his son everything he knew. Now, the son wanted to move the business in a different direction. The father didn't like this, and things were uncomfortable in the shop – so much so that the two stopped working together*

---

[8] After the Handshake, Harvard Business Review, 2016

and maintained different business hours. I remember over the holidays one year, they tried to get together for Thanksgiving, business aside – yet both shared with me afterward that their interactions felt hollow and forced given the prevailing, underlying tension that their professional relationship put on their personal one. From my perspective: the son was ready to move on and build a larger, more relevant book of clients; the father was not willing to move forward or let go. With a lack of direction and succession planning, no timeline for ownership transfer, and an unclear exit strategy, the two found themselves in an all-too-familiar scenario in which the business suffered, their relationship was frayed, and there was no clear pathway ahead.

The bottom line is this: you need to get out of the way. A new chapter is waiting to be written for your company, with a pen that you no longer hold. Your business can survive and succeed without you, but you need to help create a plan, support the hand-off, and then - as countless studies and examples offer us - move on. A business that suffers due to a leader overstaying their welcome is a business that does not have a bright, prosperous future.

And, ironically, your legacy will likely be decided for you after you leave. Do you want to guide your departure or have it be decided for you? Do you want to go on your own terms or have them dictated to you? This is the decision at hand, and it may be the most consequential of your entire business career.

A family that suffers as well

You know the saying "the elephant in the room"? Well, imagine an entire herd of elephants.

The herd? Your family.

You may have hired (and fired) some of this herd along the way (how have birthdays and Thanksgivings been, by the way?). Now, the time has come for the music to stop, for you to step aside and live a new life. What, then, for your family? Are they supportive? Or are they sharpening their knives and waiting in the bushes, ready to ambush?

They typically have your back and support you in your endeavors. Why wouldn't they? They tend to reap the benefits and rewards of your hard work. They may have helped along the way. They may have opened a few locations with you or served in senior positions. But, let's face it - they were never you. And this isn't a bad thing. They looked to you to provide and help grow the wealth and prosperity of your company and, in turn, the wealth and prosperity of the family. The past several years have benefitted them all. Yet, now that you are planning an exit, your family may wonder how this change will affect them, especially if they work in the business.

The Venn diagram of family-owned businesses consists of two things. You guessed it: family and business. Untangling the two can be a life's work in and of itself. The degree of difficulty is increased when a plan does not exist. In fact, 61% of family-owned businesses do not have a succession plan in place.[9] Another way to look at this: nearly two-thirds of family-owned businesses do not have an exit strategy, and a forced sale of the business (or its parts) may be their only option. So, look to your left and look to

---

[9] Succession-planning tips for family businesses, Royal Bank of Canada, 2024

your right: each of those fellow business owners will likely become a statistic of a failed succession, a short-lived replacement, and a rocky path ahead for business and family.

How are members of your family feeling about this lack of planning, from both a personal and a business perspective? Typically, and unfortunately, as the path forward becomes unclear, people tend to revert to a fight or flight, 'what's in it for me' mentality. And, given that 70-90% of acquisitions fail, an already confused, disjointed family, lacking any formal succession strategy or plan, find themselves reeling, buried in attorney's fees, and unsure of where to go from here, both personally and professionally.[10] It is a dismal, lonely road ahead.

The failed moment of transition casts a shadow over the family for months, sometimes years, and you cannot put the genie back in the bottle. Regardless of what happens to the business, be it a sale or some other transaction to relieve you of your duties, you will have to deal with your family, waiting for you and wanting answers. They always have. Except this time, you may not have any to give.

---

[10] The Big Idea: The New M&A Playbook, Harvard Business Review, 2016

Lost and alone

Now what?

Your family is mad at you. No course is charted for your employees, clients, or company. Your legacy is in question. How did we get here?

As we have discussed, approximately 70% of businesses do not live past the second generation. Nearly 90% of small business acquisitions fail for one reason or another. 50% of new leaders leave in the first two years of leading a new company.[11] Given the long odds against any transition, be it smooth or not, wouldn't you like to maximize the possibility that you can get out clean and clear while taking care of your people and preserving what you have built?

The feeling of being lost in all of this is not uncommon. Your whole life, you have been looked to for answers. Now, you face a question: how do you leave gracefully, support others to do your work, and become someone new? Many leaders go through this cycle of a *Hero's Journey*, where they ultimately have to confront the gaps, the facts, and themselves.

Perhaps this is less about reinventing yourself and more about repairing yourself, and your relationships, and beginning to imagine and build a new life. How do you let go of what has defined you for so long?

---

[11] Second Generation Family Leaders Don't Have It Easy, Neither Did Their Predecessors, Forbes, 2023

McKinsey's Senior Partners, who lead the Firm's CEO Excellence work, offer the following:

> *We advise CEOs to acknowledge, directly confront, and overcome the basic human fears and needs that arise when stepping down. These include losing the relevance, power, attention, and admiration that come with the job, as well as the prospect of spending time at home with a partner who has established their own rhythms and independent priorities. Add into the mix the term "retirement," which to some implies that the ravages of age and physical decline are accelerating—all of which can be mentally and emotionally difficult to embrace.*[12]

At the end of the day, however, the consequences of staying far outweigh the consequences of leaving. You have to trust this. Otherwise, you will be in a situation where the decision is made for you, and there is no worse place to be. You may not know the answer, but you can begin by living the question.

Now that we have explored the risks and ramifications of not having a fully thought-out and planned succession strategy, we can look at how to prevent the drastic and dire circumstances that befall so many business founders, owners, and leaders. The rest of this book focuses on taking deliberate, strategic steps forward for you, your family, your business, and your future. Let's begin.

---

[12] CEO Excellence, McKinsey & Co., 2024

PART 2

A Useful Guide To Overcoming The Succession Conundrum

CHAPTER 4

A Solution Awaits

"You can lead a horse to water..."

- A cowboy

The key to unlocking your future: acknowledging a plan is needed

There is a moment of tension for business owners when it becomes time to step down, step aside, or sell and move on. You may be feeling this very tension right now. *Did I do everything I set out to do? What am I leaving unfinished? Who am I leaving behind?* The truth of the matter is that when your business is struggling, you feel like you can't leave, and when it is going well, you don't want to leave. This is a dilemma faced by many - you are not alone.

Knowing it is time to step aside is perhaps the most important, and most difficult, moment in the life of a leader. Consider the sports hero at their prime or the rock star who still sells out arenas – these people are not thinking, "Maybe it's time to walk away." In many ways, you have been the star of your own show, and you may feel like you need to determine the perfect moment to leave it all behind.

The fact is, this decision is actually a series of small moments that build upon each other over the course of months and years – it is not a singular event or a lightbulb that all of a sudden goes off, and poof, just like that, you have a clear, concise succession plan and exit strategy. Not to be morbid here, but, like death, we know a date awaits us in the distant future - it chooses us. Succession is the same. At some point, we will need to move on, pass the baton, and make way for others. For many leaders who cannot plan and commit to their exit, a date chooses them, regardless of whether they have planned or not. It is inevitable - someday, perhaps in the not too distant future, your last day as owner and leader of your business will be upon you. The question is - do you want to plan for and choose that date, or do you want that date to happen to you, unannounced, forced, and unplanned?

One thing is for certain - no plan, no exit can occur without acknowledging and accepting the inevitability of transition. It is not defeat. It is an acceptance of the passage of time. The future success of your business depends on how you handle this moment. You are cementing your legacy and writing the story of the future of your business. You cannot do this without accepting that this story will carry on without you and that your chapter is coming to a close.

Visualize two pathways ahead:

> On the first path, you stay in your business too long, and you do not make room for others to grow and succeed you. The business plateaus, and when you do eventually leave, people are not sure where to go, how to lead, or what to do. Your best intentions backfired. You were the pitcher who stayed in too long, the singer who performed too late - sadly, you overstayed your welcome.
>
> Now, on the other path, you created a well-thought-out, integrated succession plan to pave the way for a smooth transition and exit for you, a solid step-up for members of your business, family, or a possible buyer, and the growth and success of the business in your absence. You are appreciated and celebrated, your business flourishes, and your smooth transition leads you to a business afterlife of new beginnings, perspective, and joy.

We likely agree on which path you would prefer, but at the outset, at the fork in the road of decision-making, how do you know when, or even if, you have taken the right turn to lead you to this reality above? What is needed for you, and those around you, to be absolutely sure you are on the right path?

The rest of this book is the "How To" – how to accept the moment, how to rise to it with a plan, and how to ensure the effects of doing both will have a significant, positive impact on the people and things you cherish the most. First and foremost, acknowledgment unlocks and unleashes the capabilities of others, and only when you accept the moment, and the decision, can you begin to plan and prepare for it. Preparation is key. The plan is key. These are the ingredients to a successful send-off - for your legacy, business, family, and future.

Your roadmap out: creating a strong succession plan

We keep referring to a plan. Let me be clear - you could have a one-page succession plan, and it would likely solve 80% of your transition woes. Maybe 70% if you have some sneaky family members waiting in the shadows to ambush you once you announce your decision.

When I left my business, my plan was six pages. I shared it with my board and staff, sanitized it for the public, and managed against it for six months. And then, as I had written and promised, I was gone. No e-mail access, no log-in credentials, no decision-making authority. Just, gone.

I had written in my doctoral dissertation: leaders need to understand their time to step forward, step back, and step out.[13] I committed to and lived this, both in my leadership over the course of a decade and in my final act as founder. Step forward, step back, step out. How you spend your time across these three actions will define you, as it did me.

The only reason I was able to do this was because of a strong succession plan. This document served as a roadmap and

---

[13] Contemplating Kuleana, ALTERNATIVE, 2009

framework for all things me, my business, the past, and the future. While these may not be the only components of a good succession plan, they drove mine, and they were highly effective.

1. The past - much of which has to be untangled and left to rest.

2. The future - waiting to be written, but only once you step foot out that door.

3. The business - will live on past you, and your true impact will be realized.

4. You - caught in between these competing elements but in charge of your destiny.

Often, when getting started on a plan, there is a tendency to allow great to be the evil of good, meaning, we feel we have to get everything perfect on the first try. This is not true, nor is it a helpful frame of reference. This mindset paralyzes us into thinking we need things just right in order to execute and make headway.

So, how do you overcome this mindset? Release yourself from striving for perfection, and instead, hold close the notion that the first step is the most important. In this context, a working plan is nearly as good as a complete one. The enemy is not imperfect completion – the enemy is not starting at all.

To make progress, we need to start somewhere, iterate versions of the plan as we live it, and integrate input along the way. This is a living, *Google Doc* version of a plan, not the final printed *PDF* for presentation.

Consider the pilot with a flight plan; if and when turbulence is forecasted, the route changes. Same destination: landing safely on the target runway. For you, your runway is a clean exit from your business while tending to the components above. In many ways, your plan must change, or else it is the past version of itself, not reflective of where you currently are on the journey towards your business afterlife.

The truth of the matter: small steps, when linked together, are what you see when you look back after crossing the finish line. You will likely not be catapulted to your exit by one, single *Hail Mary* pass, but instead by a logical, methodical ground game. Our work is the ground game, in the trenches, and it sometimes feels like we are not making progress. However, the small, nimble movements toward the ultimate destination are what matter. This is how you build your plan. This is how you survive. This is how you get out.

Executing the plan, living its benefits, and adjusting along the way

Deciding you need a plan and creating the plan are only half the battle. Then, you have to live the plan. You have to actually do what you determined would be the best course of action for you, your family, and your company. Otherwise, it is just an exercise. A document that lives and dies as fast as it was written.

I know what you are thinking: I'll just hold onto this plan as a failsafe, put it on the shelf for when I am actually ready to step aside, or save it as an eject button if and when things go sideways. A succession plan does not work that way. It is not an evacuation plan out of a burning building, nor can it just be turned on. It is a living, breathing, organic set of steps and intentions that must be lived, experienced, and implemented with fidelity. Otherwise, it is simply like any other document posted on the Internet for Google or ChatGPT to spit back to you when you need it.

Execution of the plan is the input and it is the intention; the benefit of the plan is the result and the outcome. Once you commit to making use of and implementing a strong, intentional, strategic course of action, you will begin to see and realize the results and implications of such planning and purpose. Small steps will lead to progress; progress will begin to illuminate the path ahead, and ultimately, the light at the end of the tunnel (it is not a train by the way; it is the beach, the mountains, your grandkids, fishing, reading, gardening, and the thousand other things that are waiting for you). Progress allows you to take stock in what is increasingly changing from the present to the past, and it allows you to better picture and realize your future.

And, along the way, you will be required to adjust. You will be required to change direction in preparation for or response to challenges that come your way. Obstacles will appear. Off-ramps to your plan may seem more appealing.

Waiting on forever – I had a client who made incredible apple and pumpkin pies from a secret family recipe. They had been working for two years on developing a relationship with a major wholesaler, and they were led to believe they would be heavily featured in an upcoming holiday dessert campaign across hundreds of stores nationwide, likely leading to a trajectory-changing boost in production, sales, and profitability. My client wanted to see the campaign take off, while her kids wanted her to retire, as she had committed to already - "Mom, this is a mirage and you may not find water," they told her. To this day, the wholesaler has not picked up her product. My client is still working, waiting for her big breakthrough – a breakthrough that may never come, while her kids - and the business - are waiting on her.

There will always be another exciting opportunity right around the corner that will delay your exit and the future success of the business. Mentally prepare for these moments by expecting their inevitability. Settle your mind and heart as you imagine the road ahead. And that is so much of this - visualizing the path ahead of you, as you have done so many times before in the course of your business. See the path, imagine the finish line, and do not allow the headwinds of the journey to turn you back. Do not allow the promise of future business possibilities to keep you in the throes of the day-to-day business life that you are trying so hard to move forward from. What is at stake is too important, and you cannot risk turning back now. The true oasis is not behind you - it is just ahead.

CHAPTER 5

The Moment is Here and You Will Benefit From a New Perspective

"We cannot solve our problems with the same thinking we used when we created them."

- Albert Einstein

Change is on the horizon

You have worked your whole life. You have given to and served others. You have built a business, created jobs, and made an impact. Employees, clients, and community members have asked much of you, and now, the next biggest ask: *for you to walk away from what you have spent a life building and leading.*

Why is it so difficult to accept change in our lives? In one way, we are being asked to walk away from what we have been so good at for so long. But even good things must run their course and come to a natural end, and by accepting that it is time to close one chapter, another can open.

Leaving your role as a business owner and leader may feel like stopping. Another way to look at it: it is actually just the beginning. You have an opportunity to start the next version of who you are and who you want to become.

There are three key questions to ponder as you work to accept that change is necessary:

- How do you know it is time to walk away?
- What are the people closest to you saying about this transition?
- What is it that you are actually deciding and accepting?

First, you will know it is time to walk away when more days than not you wake up wondering what life on the other side is going to look like. When you cross that 50/50 point, it may be time to set a date. Picking a firm date will ensure that you do not allow for the winds of change and opportunity to blow you back to your comfort zone and the role that you have operated from for so long. The best founders, owners, and leaders clarify their time frames with key stakeholders well in advance and land on a specific, planned departure date – and then they commit.[14] Put simply: pick a firm date, share it, and execute around it.

Next, listen to the people in your life that love you the most. What are they telling you? Is there a common theme? The difficulty of advice is that it is not monolithic, and you will need to observe the skew of these advisors. Search, listen, contemplate, and find a resting place. This is the throughline that can and should guide

---

[14] Sending it forward: Successfully transitioning out of the CEO role, McKinsey, 2023

you. It may not be one voice, but rather the song through which all voices are coming together to sing to you. Hear this song, heed the message - it is critical advice that is timely and necessary to guide you.

Lastly, consider what it is you are actually deciding. Acknowledgment of this moment will allow you to make sense of what is about to happen, what it means for others, and what it means for you. Think about what the decision is - succession? Selling? Giving over to employees? Consider the nuances of your decision so that you can truly wrap your mind and heart around your final resting place, which should be a place of peace, on your terms and on your timeline.

Getting clear on these questions will allow you to start processing the moment and begin to formulate answers. This will in turn help you accept and acknowledge, to others and to yourself, that change is on the horizon.

A plan to navigate this change

Now that you have accepted that change is inevitable, on the near-term horizon, and you are the central figure, the protagonist if you will - now what?

Accepting the moment of change is only your buy-in; you also must know how to navigate and how to succeed. We can refer to this as your "what it takes to win" plan.

Consider the captain of a sailboat (perhaps one that you will retire to) who is charting their course to an island destination.

They have accepted that the journey is imminent. Now, they need to assess weather patterns, ocean conditions, marine traffic, and other critical elements of sailing. And then, they need to make a plan to account for all of these non-cooperative, independent moving parts. It is not as if they will follow the sail plan 100%, but they will have it as a starting point to orient themselves over the horizon.

Having a plan is critical to your succession journey for three main reasons.

First, it points forward. It orients you into the storm, through change, and towards the finish line. This orientation is critical when the headwinds and conditions feel insurmountable.

Second, it allows others to join and support you on your journey. Your pace of change, the cadence of "step away" moments, and the swiftness with which the succession pendulum swings all have to do with your plan, and this plan communicates to those most important to you that you are in fact making progress, embracing change, and facing the future.

Last, and perhaps most importantly, it is the final chapter of your business ownership and leadership experience that you will own and lead. Yes, there may be an epilogue; you may write a book of your own someday, reflecting on your experience (I would like to read it). However, right now, this is the last, central, and defining playbook that you will bring to life as a leader. Don't you want it to have a resounding and lasting impact, and to be the most successful plan yet?

Accepting change is one thing. Planning for it is another. Having a map to guide you on your journey will make all the difference.

Critical mistake: creating the plan alone

So, now you have accepted that the moment of change is here, and you have accepted that a plan is needed to navigate this change and guide you on your journey. Now, it's time to accept what is perhaps the most important piece: you cannot write this plan on your own.

Yes, you can and will play a central role in developing and implementing - living - this plan. However, if you alone write this succession plan, you will fail to take advantage of a moment when an omniscient perspective, a clean pair of hands, and a fresh set of eyes are needed. See Albert Einstein above - do you disagree with Albert?

When we write about ourselves, when we take surveys about ourselves in comparison to others, literally anytime that we are the central character of a narrative we tell ourselves, we offer ourselves a tremendous amount of grace and benefit of the doubt. We explain away our faults, justify our intentions, and view ourselves extremely favorably. This might be fine when journaling or working our way through a difficult, personal chapter of our lives. However, when our business, our employees, our family, our reputation, and our future is on the line, we need not give ourselves too much wiggle room. We need someone to tell us the truth.

How might an outside perspective benefit you at this moment?

- Providing honest, direct feedback
- Acting as a gentle sparring partner to wrestle with on difficult topics that may have previously gone unsaid
- Supporting the untangling of the past while keeping an eye on the future
- Ensuring accountability and keeping a pulse on employees, clients, and stakeholders
- Offering a degree of separation between the family while effectively liaising

These are a few of the immediate and ongoing benefits of having a succession partner and advisor who can help you see the next bounce of the ball and plan for a journey that will be like no other you have ever taken - your final ride.

Do not go it alone. Do not draft a self-serving plan that gives you grace and leaves important issues unresolved. An outside perspective offers you the opportunity to share some of the burden, relinquish some of the responsibility, and maintain a sense of objectivity; it provides balance. I would advise you to enlist smart, insightful, trusted perspectives during the most important chapter of your life. You only have one shot at this.

CHAPTER 6

How to Create a Winning Plan

"A goal without a plan is just a wish."

- Antoine de Saint-Exupéry

The succession survival guide

When you camp or head out into the wilderness, you typically have three things:

1. A plan for how to safely have fun in the wild;
2. A vision for what it will look and feel like if successful; and
3. The tools and resources necessary to achieve both.

Your plan, or *guide*, is built around the resources you take with you and the elements you will likely encounter. Weather, topography, elevation, natural surroundings, length of camp, people involved – these all matter in the best and worst scenarios you may find yourself in. Your plan must effectively match your resources with your surroundings, weaving together the situations that arise with the preparation you have completed.

The same is true for succession planning – it truly is a wilderness, one that you likely have not encountered before. In heading into this wilderness, a series of tools and frameworks will exponentially increase your odds of a smooth, effective transition away from your business.

Three key themes comprise this guide and drive successful succession planning, and these themes happen across complimentary time horizons. Picture, on the vertical y-axis: you, your business, and everything else. And then, on the horizontal x-axis, picture the past, the present, and the future. You now have nine boxes, and for each, you need to strategize. These nine boxes may not be the only areas you need to solve in order to hack through the succession wilderness. But they cover significant ground and will give you visibility into critical areas that will affect your survival. They are, in part, the keys to helping you get out alive.

(See next page for framework)

The Succession Survival Guide[15]

	BEFORE	DURING	AFTER
SELF The transitioning leader	**100-Day Plan** featuring alignment, organizational choreography, and instructional stakeholder investment[1]	**Real-time coaching and "bat phone"** support for leader through most critical moments of succession	**Continued transition support** as leader shifts from out front to sideline advisor, ensuring gentle swing of leadership pendulum
BUSINESS The company and internal stakeholders	**Business Transition Plan** for the organization including operational, organizational, financial, and other go-forward considerations to ensure resilience	**Execution** of corresponding (a) 100-Day Plan and (b) Business Transition Plan to ensure consistent, choreographed hand-over of leadership and business direction	**Growth strategy support** including strategic planning, governance (re)structuring, leadership development, and transition execution
EVERYTHING ELSE External stakeholders and factors	**Landscape analysis** of the current business ecosystem, economic outlook, competitors, policy implications, and more	**Ongoing monitoring,** assessment, and response to various external "ripple effect" implications from transition while calming stakeholders	**Re-engaging external** opportunities as a former leader while seeking positive community impact

First and foremost, you. You are the central character – the protagonist – of your journey. Understanding and executing a plan for yourself will offer the highest return and ripple effect outward to your employees, clients, families, and beyond. Creating a 100-day plan (at the very minimum – it could be up to two years, or more), and managing this plan throughout your succession

---

[15] Version 1.0

period, is one of the central elements that will help orient all other components.

Next, your business. How do you ensure that your business doesn't become one of the vast majority that fail because of poor succession planning? The solution has to do with creating the conditions for a positive trajectory for the future after you are gone. A solid Business Transition Plan that points to sustainable growth after your departure is a central, enabling component to this positive trajectory. Remember, your true legacy is earned in your absence, whether you prefer it or not.

Last, everything else. Clients, competitors, unions, media, creditors... everyone will line up and want their shot at you. Controlling the narrative and calmly, strategically getting ahead of the wave of pressure that is coming will ensure you are owning all that you can through the closing moments of your tenure. Passing it off is not an option, and you have never pointed to anyone else your entire life to handle tough moments - this is yours to guide. Your business afterlife is close, but stay the course and manage the ripple of information and communication that can serve as a wave of momentum through the finish.

The Succession Survival Guide will help you pack up and critically prepare for the journey ahead. In other words, it will help you determine when to hold on, and when to let go. Next, we talk about how to separate what is business and what is personal. It may not be a clear line, but learning how to navigate the Venn diagram that you likely find yourself in will make all the difference.

Separate the business from the personal, the past from the future

Picture a four-circle Venn diagram that offers the following elements: you, your business, the past, and the future. We refer to this as the Succession Kaleidoscope, a viewpoint of overlapping perspectives and states of being. Similar to the Succession Survival Guide above, it allows us to zero in on areas of tension and explore the opportunities they create. As one lens shifts and moves towards another, it creates an area - or moment - for us to explore. Correspondingly, as the lens moves, it affects another area of the kaleidoscope. All areas are separate; and at the same time, all areas are interrelated. No one area can shift without having an impact on the rest.

Succession Kaleidoscope

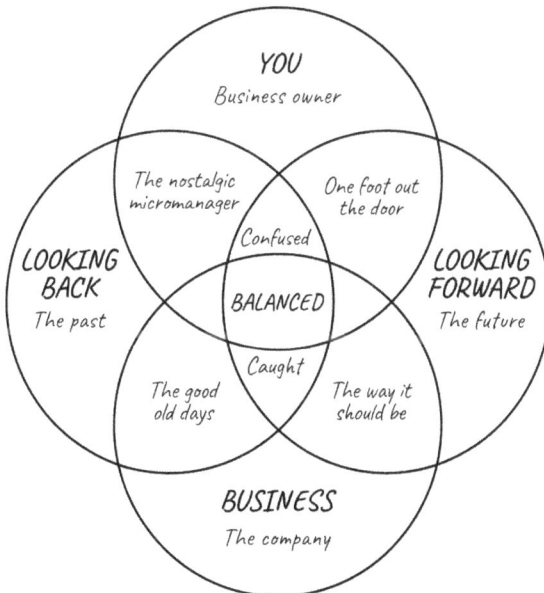

Let's double-click a few of the stickiest, most challenging areas of overlap; the areas that make you say, "No, those are fine, I got those," while trying hard to ignore the pit in your stomach.

My guess is these are the three:

1. You and the future
2. The business and the future
3. The center where everything meets

Let's break these down one by one. The future, for you, is wide open. This is what, ironically, gives CEOs and business leaders the most pause. You have been responsible for and in charge of so much for so long - what happens when the music stops?

> *The Small Things – A few years ago, a former client left her CEO position after 15 years at the helm. She had taken over for her father, who had taken over for his father – there was a century-old legacy riding on her daily decisions and leadership, and the weight became too much. COVID, A.I., online competition, and a changing workforce – she was done. Her biggest worry, the night before she logged off, was: "Who will make sure the employee of the month picture is framed?" Seriously. Multi-million dollar company, dozens and dozens of colleagues, years of client relationships and legacy – her concern was a monthly picture. It can be that simple, but the absence of responsibility, in some ways, can feel heavier in those final days than the culmination of all those years before.*

In some ways, the music is just starting. You are getting another chance to be you, albeit with a few gray hairs. Your family, your hobbies, your passions - your life. It is time to move on.

The flip side of this is your business. There is so much that only you know how to do — that you have done already. You may stay up at night wondering who is going to close deals, nurture relationships, and keep the peace. But just because it was you in the past, it doesn't mean it is you in the future. In fact, respectfully, it can't be.

If Drew Bledsoe never got hurt, we wouldn't know Tom Brady. Without the competition from Blackberry, Apple may not have ever been so driven to create the iPhone. Each and every moment of our past has happened for a reason, and now, our present is moving us forward through this place in time, allowing for someone else, something else to take over. For the sake of your business, this means accepting that life will go on without you. It must.

For you, it also means letting go. You may struggle with certain the elements in the Succession Kaleidoscope. What feels most personal to you will likely be the hardest to plan around. This is also why it is critical to enlist the help and perspective of others, of trusted advisors, of people who know and want what is best for you to help you make progress towards your goals.

You can solve for 90% of what will keep you up at night with a good plan. It takes a working framework and the ability to lean into the areas of tension that will trip you up and hold you back. Progress is possible, but you - and others - need to commit to it.

Increase your odds of success

The "Pareto Principle," also known as the *80/20 rule,* states that 20% of the causes produce 80% of the outcomes. In other words, you might increase your effectiveness by four times (4x) if you focus on the right one fifth of anything you do. There are caveats to this, of course; however, the idea remains that focusing on the right causes will lead to maximized outcomes.

Now, let's make it relevant to you, in succession planning terms. Say there are 100 things you need to do in order to effectively move on and complete your succession. Only 20 of those 100 actions will produce at least 80% of the overall impact needed for your plan. Do you know which 20 those are? Do they affect you, your business, your team, or your family? Are they evenly split?

A team and a perspective that helps you (a) imagine, (b) create, and (c) execute the most important 20% of succession responsibilities is critical to the plan. When you know which responsibilities are in the top 20% and which areas of the plan they affect, you can ensure your effort is maximized, not wasted.[16]

Additionally, your plan can and should have other people - your team of advisors and consigliere - built into the cadence of execution. Ironically, the more you focus on and welcome others to the plan, the easier it will be to swing the pendulum away from you and towards them. I coach my clients to form what I refer to as their "trail team." Call this the team of advisors, the transition

---

[16] How to Plan for a Business Exit, Cresset Capital, 2024

team, or the new management; however you view these people, they are critical to your success.

Lastly, ensuring progress against this plan requires accountability. This trail team is the group that will hold you accountable, and their input must be welcomed. The challenge, of course, is that it may have been the other way around for many years. Now, they have to tell you what to do, by when, etc. Three things can help with this rebalance of authority and direction:

1. Choose a firm exit date to strategize around;
2. Publicly state efforts and key elements of the plan to benchmark against; and
3. Welcome an external perspective to serve as an objective, win-oriented guide through the process.

The plan, the team, the elements of progress - these are all necessary to move you on an efficient journey towards your business afterlife. At the end of the day, your execution is only as good as your plan, team, and willingness to commit and execute.

Short and sweet is the recipe for success

My doctoral dissertation all came down to a diagram drafted on a paper towel; seriously. Three years, 146 pages, a newly formed organization, hundreds of people, dozens of employees - one chicken-scratched grid with some notes on a napkin dotted with pasta sauce.

Anyone who tells you there is a correlation between how pretty a plan is and its effectiveness is lying or trying to sell you something.

What matters is if it works. Nearly two thirds of CEO successions at the largest companies in the world are planned,[17] but the inverse is true for small businesses, with 6 out of 10 not having a succession plan in place.[18]

Writing and executing my own plan over the course of several months; working alongside Senior Partners at McKinsey to craft strategies for CEO exits of major Fortune 100 companies; supporting my own family's business through succession and sale; going to school, over and over again, to learn about how the best businesses in the world grew, and stopped growing — the world of *getting out* has far more similarities than you might think. Even now, as I help clients with their own, unique succession planning needs, I see owners face the same obstacles and lean on the same win strategies to find their way out of the wilderness – and that truly is what it is: a succession wilderness.

Now that you have elements of a plan for surviving the wilderness, we will focus on key aspects of execution that can help further increase your odds of success, both now and after this succession process is over. A plan is only as good as its owner's ability to execute. We have the why and the what; now comes the how.

---

[17] What happens after a legendary CEO departs, Strategy&, 2024
[18] Succession-planning tips for family businesses, Royal Bank of Canada, 2024

CHAPTER 7

Executing the Plan and Living Its Benefits

"It is easier to put on a pair of shoes than to wrap the earth in leather."

- Chögyam Trungpa

The first step is the hardest one

Remember when you first started your business? Or started leading your business? The early days when you showed up and asked: "What am I doing? What should I be doing?" One thing led to another, and soon, you could not find the time each day to handle the people, tasks, and fires that came your way.

The early days and the first steps are the hardest. These are often when first impressions are made – some that last, and some that don't. Vision and ideas meet planning and execution, but those early moments also come with inertia. It is often easier, and perhaps less risky, to turn back and into the comfort of the norm. But the norm wasn't what your business was built on. The norm was the 9 out of 10 entrepreneurs that couldn't get their venture off the ground or closed up shop because they couldn't find a path forward.

Why? What holds us back from taking these first steps towards the finish line of our business days and toward the starting line of our new, reimagined lives? For some, the glory days of owning and managing are close in the rearview; too close perhaps. For others, there may be unfinished business, or one final act to solidify the perception of their own legacy. These thoughts serve as the centrifugal force away from the central, focal point of your entire business life - the end of one chapter and the beginning of another. Denying this change is futile, and acknowledging that the early moments will be the hardest can help you overcome them.

Let it Breathe – A client recently shared a story of his father's wine business, and a stand-off his father had with his brother, my client's uncle, nearly 40 years ago. The father and uncle had diverging views of how the business should evolve. Whether to maintain tradition and honor heritage, explore new techniques, grow from small-batch production in search of better economics for their vineyard – they could not seem to find common ground. My client's father ended up relinquishing his managerial authority in a partial buy-out, but maintained an ownership stake in the winery. Their continued disagreement denied progress for the winery, and eventually, they sold to a competitor.

Looking back, my client would say of the situation: they should have just let it breathe. Similar to the wines they had made for so many years, my client's father could have stepped away and allowed his brother to fully lead the winery down a different path than one he would have chosen. Had he taken those initial steps away, perhaps he would have brought resolution to the situation, and both brothers and the winery would have been successful. While those first steps would have been the hardest, they would have also been the most consequential.

What is at stake here can be broken into three key messages you can remind yourself of over and over as you enter this phase:

1. If you don't move on, neither can anyone else;
2. Your business is ready for a new leader - do not let it, and others, suffer; and
3. The life you can and will live will not wait forever.

Consider the personal, business, and "everything else" buckets of our Succession Survival Guide, and ask yourself across each - what are you hanging on to? What is holding you back? What is at stake if you begin your transition? What is at stake if you don't? Starting is the hardest part. The first few steps are the most important and also the most difficult.

Small steps forward lead to big progress

Once you have made up your mind and committed to setting your succession plan in motion, it is important to build momentum. A succession task a day keeps the doctor away, or something like that. Jim Collins referred to the flywheel effect, whereas energy and effort lead to momentum, which in turn carries you forward, for a certain amount of time.[19] The output is the distance you cover towards your exit; the inputs are your actions. And your actions are critical.

Three recommendations might help with making immediate, sustained progress:

1. Chunk the succession actions - Rome wasn't built in a day, and you do not have to complete your entire plan at once; break the major pieces up into smaller, more manageable sections or phases (an advisor or transition team can help with this);

2. Make your intentions and actions public - this way, you have already committed to completing a task (e.g., announcing your exit date, putting forth a slate of successors, hiring a lawyer or business broker for due diligence in a possible sale, meeting with key clients to discuss their future relationship with your company). This will make all the difference once you know others are counting on you to deliver - you always have; and

3. Calendar key milestones - The first and most important milestone is a firm exit date. After this, work backwards and plan smaller, more manageable milestones that will allow you to build a rhythm and cadence of succession wins.

---

[19] Good to Great, Collins, 1990

These tasks above may feel tall and insurmountable as you navigate the conflicting emotions and various demands on your time and attention. The good news: a team can help. A transition team composed of a few key figures (e.g., attorney, banker, advisor) can help chunk, announce, and calendar your actions in a way that feels far more approachable.

Remember the 100-day plan from above? This is where a 30-60-90 day (or longer) series of time horizons can help break down the complex task of unwinding your leadership position into more manageable, tactical actions that can be accomplished collectively.

And now, as you find yourself executing these tasks towards the finish line, it is important to take stock of and celebrate the progress and momentum.

Take stock in progress towards the door

Why does it matter to celebrate progress? Maybe you never congratulated anyone until the job was done. But this is different. It is not self-serving or aggrandizing. It is an opportunity for you to memorialize the critical transition moments and to allow others closure as you pass the torch.

While it may go without saying, stepping aside gracefully and effectively is critical to the success of your people, company, and clients. We all know the cautionary tales of leaders who are ousted, owners who are bought out, and folks who just quit. Their energy and impact reverberates throughout the company and lingers, like a fog, into the future.

Leaving on good terms helps you, your people, your team, your family, and ultimately, your future. Closing the door amicably supports you in embracing what is next. Only by leaving a trail of light and positivity, and celebrating the journey, can you set the foundation for what is to come. Successors of longstanding CEOs typically have shorter tenures and worse financial performance, and they're often forced out.[20] Your leaving matters, and how you do it matters even more.

> *A Simple Note – a recent client left his company and sent handwritten notes to his employees, no matter their rank and tenure, and flowers to their spouses. You would not imagine the response he got. For months, people found him (he had changed his number, e-mail, and mailing address) to thank him and share the effect. Not only did this have an incredibly positive impact on the people who he left the business to - it made him feel good to celebrate those who he had traveled this journey with for so long. Ultimately, it helped him find a sense of closure across the relationships he had held close for so long.*

Taking stock of your progress, celebrating wins along the way, leaving with care, and acknowledging the people you will eventually, and respectfully, move on from allows for a gentle and meaningful swing of the pendulum - away from your past, toward your future. The way you leave, and the manner in which you treat people on the way out, makes all the difference - for you, for them, and for the business.

---

[20] Beware the Transition from an Iconic CEO, Harvard Business Review, 2023

PART 3

The Future You Deserve

CHAPTER 8

Changing Direction, Staying The Course

"Unless commitment is made, there are only promises and hopes; but no plans."

- Peter Drucker

Challenges and changes in direction will occur - mentally prepare now

It is not a matter of if, but when, a challenge or setback to your succession plan will occur. Beyond the struggle of deciding, planning, and executing your succession strategy, moments will arise during which you ask yourself, "is this the right course of action?"

> *A line in the sand – A recent client, an Executive Director, shared that her board initially pressed her when she confidentially shared her intention to sunset her term. The board chair said, "Wouldn't it be easier if you just*

finished out the fiscal year and then took a year to plan?"
While a longer timeline may very well have been more
organizationally beneficial, her broader life plans did not
allow her the luxury to take 12-18 months to transition.
She ended up announcing her date, sticking to it, and has
not second-guessed her decision since.

These setback moments tend to appear in three forms: (1) voices, (2) what-ifs, and (3) better-offs. If unprepared, significant mental and emotional capacity is required across each of these to push through.

The voices come from people, and typically those who are closest to you. They are not your team of aligned advisors who are committed to the vision of you stepping back, succeeding, and moving on. They are your friends, board members, colleagues, co-founders - they are people who don't want you to leave. Like the Sirens of Odysseus, their voices sing to you in hopes that you will leave the course you have charted for some other reality. We do not always know their intentions, and the more time we spend trying to figure them out, the less time we spend executing our plan to move forward and get out.

What ifs are scenarios you play in your head across any number of situations. These are missed deals and opportunities right around the corner, people who may step up, competitors who may falter - the what ifs are all of the trade-offs that go through your mind as you slowly walk towards the door and seek to close this chapter of your life. These what-ifs have always been there, but now, as you seek to move on, they possess a different kind of gravity that begs your attention. They create a mirage, and they can lead you astray to a land of what might have been, not what is, or what could be in your post-business life.

Lastly, when you start to wonder if you have made the right choice and your decisions begin to echo in your mind, this is the "am I better off?" moment. If what-ifs offer the F.O.M.O. and possible opportunity cost of moving on, better-offs cast doubt on your decision and force you to juxtapose the possibility of a future life with the reality of the one you live. You question if the grass is greener, whether you will be happy in your business afterlife, and if you will truly, wholly be better off.

The good news is that preparation and priming yourself for these challenges can help you address and even get ahead of the situations that are sure to arise. Keeping a team of advisors close to help you on this journey can help you see around the corner. On this team of advisors, you don't want people who are telling you what you want to hear, but true partners who can spar with and support you as you progress. Subtle changes in strategy are often necessary, and these can be done proactively.

Settle your mind and heart for the transition

Being in a challenging situation as a protagonist, which you are, is incredibly difficult when you cannot see yourself from an omniscient point of view, and when you can't accurately plot yourself between being balanced and being in a state of disequilibrium.

In a dynamic leadership guide developed by two professors out of the Harvard Kennedy School, the authors explore many critical leadership mindsets and frameworks, two of which are critical to keeping a settled mind and heart in the midst of a leadership transition.[21]

The first is what the authors refer to as "getting on the balcony." In succession, there are so many swirling, moving pieces - you, your business, employees, clients, competitors, creditors, family members, and family members who might act as creditors... Imagine you are on a dance floor, and you are all swirling and moving around, interconnected. Now, try to see the patterns. From the floor, it is nearly impossible. Instead, you have to (you guessed it) move to the balcony to get a bird's eye view of the totality of the group, their movements, patterns that emerge, and insights you can act on.

The second, and perhaps the most critically important leadership coaching tool I have ever used, is the "productive zone of disequilibrium." The concept highlights a range in which we operate that is above our avoidant, deferential treatment of issues and below the limit of tolerance, above which we are unproductive due to stress, emotion, lack of logic - you name it. Staying in this productive range takes incredible discipline, commitment in the moment, and constant mindfulness about the challenges at hand.

---

[21] Leadership on the Line, Heifetz and Linsky, 2002

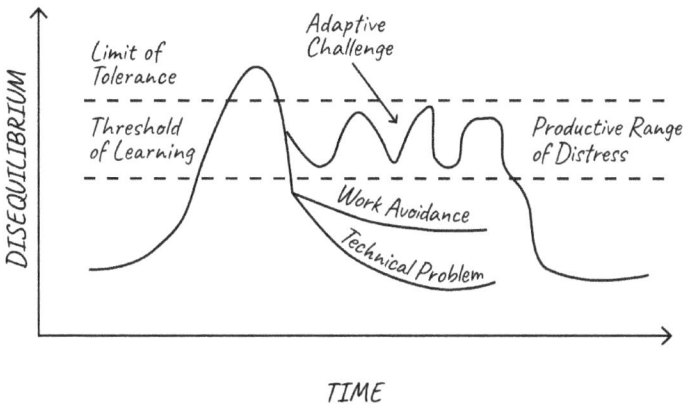

Source: Ronald A. Heifetz and Donald C. Laurie, "Mobilizing Adaptive Work:
Beyond Visionary Leadership," in Jay A. Conger, Gretchen M. Spreitzer, and
Edward E. Lawler III, eds., The Leader's Change Handbook: an Essential Guide
to Setting Direction and Taking Action (New York: John Wiley & Sons, 1998)

Consider something: this may be the first and last time you ever
leave your own company. What strategies will you integrate into
this moment of leaving your business and position? What sense
are you making of it all, and how are you handling yourself in the
distress? Only by settling your mind and heart, acknowledging the
challenging moments you will find yourself in, and maintaining
balance will you make your way through the storm that is
succession. And make it through you will, so long as you don't
turn back.

The finish line is the starting line - do not turn back now

Imagine training for years to compete in your first triathlon. All
of the miles logged, your fitness and health, training partners and
team, your bike. Now, imagine you get up the day of the race, get

ready to swim, and just before the gun goes off, all of the voices and thoughts of what could go wrong, or what you might be missing, creep into your head – there could be sharks in the water, your bike won't hold up, you can't complete a marathon. As the gun sounds, you turn back, hop in the car, and go home.

The finish line of your training is the start of the race. These two chapters of your life are separated by one thin line and one moment: a person training for a triathlon, and a triathlete.

The finish line for your succession plan is the start of your new life, post-business, and a chapter that is waiting to be written. Folks who turn back into the fold as they near the exit perhaps get cold feet at the notion they will be irrelevant. Shortly after leaving office, former U.S. President Harry Truman said, "Two hours ago, I could have said five words and been quoted in every capital of the world. Now, I could talk for two hours, and nobody would give a damn."[22] In one moment, everything changes.

We have mentioned multiple strategies and frameworks for you to leverage in order to build momentum toward the finish line of your plan. However, getting past that final obstacle, the *Hillary Step* of your succession journey will require you to do three things: (1) commit, (2) plan, and (3) sever.

Your first step is to know, commit, and communicate the date. Earlier, we discussed having a date to plan around. Now, this date is for you to execute upon. Know this date, not just for others, but for yourself. Treat it like a wedding, a flight leaving, a court

---

[22] H. F. Graff, "When the term's up, it's better to go gracefully," International Herald Tribune, January 26, 1988

date - know, calendar, commit to, and honor this date. It is a critical milestone.

Second, make serious plans and commitments in the days, weeks, and months following your departure date. Maybe this is that deferred trip to Italy with your spouse, coaching your granddaughter's softball team, or joining a local non-profit board. Fill your calendar with your future. Set tangible, near-term, non-revocable commitments to others.

Lastly, and in all seriousness, ask the HR and tech folks at your company to immediately sever your phone, e-mail, key access, and credentials on your final day. Treat yourself like any other employee who has come and gone. With little to no fanfare, throw your keys on your desk. Make the small, typically unseen hand-off of access and availability a planned, programmed step in the process. You cannot imagine the freedom you will feel when your e-mail and business phone are turned off. It will be the final forcing mechanism to let you know: it's over. Again, tee up someone else to be responsible to ensure this gets done. Don't put this on your final to-do list - it may not be that easy when you are faced with the finality of it all.

As you near the finish line, there are two similar, critical questions to ask: what is at stake if I go? What is at stake if I stay? Likely, you have asked variations of these questions along the way. However, this is when it truly matters, and you need to increasingly focus on the downside of staying and the upside of leaving. You have advisors to help you, a plan to guide you, and a calendar of opportunities waiting for you right on the other side of that date. Now, you just need to stay the course.

CHAPTER 9

Light on the Horizon

"You can't start the next chapter of your life if you keep re-reading the last one."

- Unknown

Your business will take off without you - and that's okay

Imagine for a minute that you have finally made it to the finish line, or the starting line, as it were. Your last day has come and gone, your email is shut off, your phone number is changed, and access to the building – denied.

Feels good, doesn't it? Totally and completely disconnected. On one hand, you may be thinking: who is going to handle that one situation with a certain client that only I know how to do? Or, what happens if there is a crisis that only I know how to fix?

Chances are, if you built and executed a strong succession plan with a trusted team of advisors, your business is already well into its next chapter. Have you ever heard of an S-curve graph?

There is a brief moment when a new transition leads to a dip in productivity, output, or success. There is an isolated, temporary period of decline – decline in institutional knowledge, efficiency, and accomplishment. But then, as momentum takes hold, growth is experienced above and beyond the maximum possible from before. Only by allowing for that temporary decline and starting anew can your company exceed what was previously possible.

We have seen this with sports teams over and over again. No one could have imagined that Boston would trade gold glove Nomar Garciaparra in 2004 after coming within an inning of the World Series the year before. But what did they do – traded him to the Cubs at the deadline, and Boston won the World Series for the first time in 86 years that fall. Only through a period of brief decline could new players step up and a new culture form to take the team to the promised land.

And the same goes for business. The only way a company can grow past its previous expectations and potential is by resetting the business cycle, stepping down or back for a moment, only to build new momentum and find a way forward, past what was previously possible.

You need to imagine your business post-you to truly understand what is possible in this next chapter. You need to set in motion and unlock the next S-curve.

Typical Business Cycle

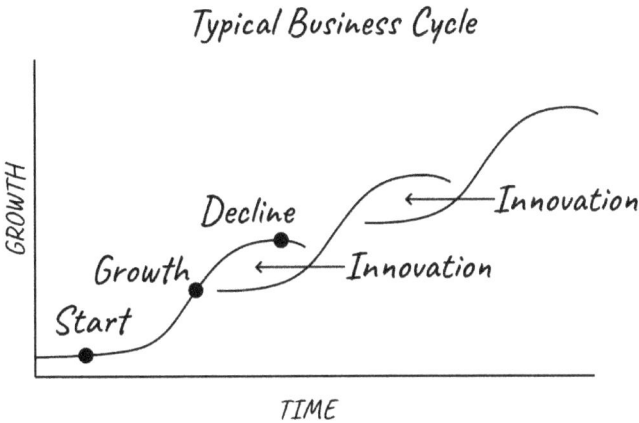

Consider for a moment, three different scenarios:

- The first, you stayed, and the business eventually leveled off or even declined due to your focus shifting elsewhere;
- The second, you left without a plan, and everyone had to scramble and pick up the pieces; and
- The third, you planned, executed, and handed off the business into a positive trajectory and into a key inflection point for refreshed leadership, thinking, and growth.

Your business will be fine, and it will likely thrive in your absence, if properly prepared. In fact, your leaving may unlock the next stage of growth and success for the company. Know that you play a key role in ensuring a smooth, impactful hand-off to the next cadre of leadership, and by leaving, you not only release the business from your shadow, but you provide the necessary permission and opportunity for others to step up and lead.

It is the last, and perhaps most important, leadership move you can make. It is a selfless act, and it will make all the difference for your people. People have followed you for years - decades, in some instances. It is now time for them to lead themselves. You must go, and they cannot follow this time.

Your people will be okay - trust them

When I ask my clients, "What is one of the biggest things you are worried about once you leave?", they say: their people. When I ask, "Who are your people?", they say: everyone. Employees, clients, family, old bosses, legacy competitors - everyone.

Likewise, after they leave their post, an enormous sense of weight comes off their shoulders. For some, it is guilt that they didn't do more. For others, it is a relief they no longer have to cut paychecks and feed mouths.

People are taken care of, and you might be surprised who steps up to fill the void. Who was standing on the sideline that is now thriving, leading, calling the shots? Remember the "if Bledsoe never got hurt, we might never have known Tom Brady?" thought from before?

This is true with your leadership, your team, and people within your business that you may never have imagined could blossom in your absence. Christine Daaé from Phantom of the Opera; Steve Jobs replacing Michael Scott at Apple. The point is – your business can and will thrive *if you let it*. Likewise, and read this at least once - your people will thrive too, if you let them.

In a past life, I founded, ran, and stepped down and away from a public charter school in the Hawaiian Islands with a group of fellow Teach For America alumni. After a decade of leadership, when I announced my forthcoming departure, people had mixed emotions. Some were shocked. Others were sad and disappointed. In my farewell message, I wrote the following:

> *As I step aside, the voices, vision, and leadership of my colleagues, our students, and our community will truly breathe life and energy into the mission of this school. And only by me doing so can we truly see and realize the potential of what this organization can be.*

The businesses and lives we lead as founders and owners must come to a natural conclusion at some point in order for others to begin the next chapter. And, if we have done our job correctly, the chapter that is about to be written, in our absence, will be the best one yet. You must trust that your legacy will truly be defined, and proven, once you are gone.

Your family will be at peace as well. Once you have slowed your pace and taken the CEO hat off (and not just for weekends or the occasional vacation), you can come back to your family in a way. Your spouse, kids, relatives, close friends, neighbors - all the people who blurred into the background as you built what you built. And now, with a bit of openness - and perhaps forgiveness, on both sides - you will begin to thaw relationships that have been waiting for far too long. Perhaps you were able to maintain an exact balance throughout the years, but chances are that you have some work to do. Now, you have the time to do so. Now, you can take care of people in a different way, including yourself.

Ensuring that people are taken care of means leaving your business and showing up for your family. This exchange is a natural rebalancing of your time, energy, and presence. Capitalize on it; it will only happen once. Enjoy it; it is your future, and it is waiting for you.

For you, it is finally time to move on

You made it. You completed your business succession. Maybe you sold. Maybe you passed it down to a family member. Maybe you turned off the lights for the final time. No matter what you did, you are out, and you made it to the end. Or, as we keep mentioning, the beginning.

As you cross that finish line and begin your new life, I encourage you to do three things (and I complete this with my clients):

1. Journal. Years from now, someone will want to know what you were thinking, feeling, and living through these moments. Write them down - you will be glad you did.

2. Log out. E-mails, accounts, phones, alerts - cold turkey, cut it all out. You will feel a weight lift off your shoulders, and you especially need to do this to achieve closure.

3. Travel. Or change the scenery somehow. You have been operating at a certain frequency for years, perhaps decades. Change it up, mix it up, and reset with a different horizon - you will be glad you did when you return home.

For some, the break is clean. They move on, or literally move, and get past this moment with ease and grace. For some, it is messy and takes time. There is no right or wrong, but just know that the hard part is behind you, and now it is time to live on and into the future version of you.

Your legacy is set - there's nothing you can do about it now, so no use worrying. Your business is fine - we covered that earlier. Your people, family, and the others - they are okay, too.

Now, it's you. Just you. Lonely in one sense, incredibly freeing in another. Now, all that is left to do is ask yourself: what am I doing to truly ensure my peace of mind, and to ensure that I have fully, absolutely moved on?

Exhale. Don't look back. Look forward to the chapter waiting for you. It's ready, and so are you.

CHAPTER 10

The Promised Land

"Every new beginning comes from some other beginning's end."

- Seneca

Healing and closure is required to move on

The business is in the rearview. The deal is done. Your employees have moved on. And now, you need to as well.

The early days and weeks will fade into your new existence. New habits and rituals. A new phone number and email. Perhaps a few people reach out, but overall, you are experiencing a new anonymity that you haven't had in years - decades even. It feels strange.

Two important thresholds must now be crossed to complete the journey of leaving your business – (1) healing and (2) closure.

Whereas you may have been a tough, formidable leader in a past life, the act of healing requires vulnerability and new skills and mindsets, some of which you may not have honed over the years. The very word vulnerability may be foreign to you, but you know what – the act of healing isn't just about you. Now, I am not saying go out and write letters to the people you have wronged or go on a self-pity apology tour. On the contrary – it is time for you to look in the mirror, think about what needs to be fixed, what work needs to be done, and to do it. Not just for you, but for them - your family, your spouse, the people who will always count on you, no matter your title. The act and acceptance of healing is an incredible strength, and you must exercise it, or work to build it.

Only by allowing and practicing healing will you bring closure to the previous life you once lived. The lawyers, bankers, and advisors – they have already moved on, closed your deal, and are on to the next one. But you – your experience was personal. Only by allowing healing, and practicing the act of becoming whole, can you begin to reach forward into your future to grasp what awaits you. None of the future life experiences will accept someone who has open wounds and is partly stuck in the past.

In the book *Shantaram*, there is a defining moment when one of the main characters states:

> I think that we all, each one of us, we all have to earn our future... if we don't earn it, we don't have a future at all. And if we don't earn it, we don't deserve it, and we have to live in the present, more or less forever. Or worse, we have to live in the past.[23]

---

[23] Shantaram, Gregory David Roberts, 2003

You have earned this moment, and you must move on and live your future. It is waiting for you.

Your business afterlife holds incredible impact for others

In your business afterlife, there are two routes that you can take, with some variation. One route is one of peace and quiet, tranquility, and connection with self. Another is a life of service – joining boards, volunteering, and getting civically engaged. Both have their advantages and can offer tremendous fulfillment. However, so that you don't go back down the rabbit hole of being overbooked and overwhelmed, it is important to get clear on a few things. Let's think of these as rings, or ripples, as you might see in a pond when throwing a rock into the water.

The closest and most accentuated ring or ripple is yourself. This is deeply personal reflective work that you will embark on – a journey of self-re-discovery in a way. It's not like you are going to travel the world as a Wanderlust yogi; rather, you may start reading some self-development books, speaking to a counselor or life coach, gardening, fishing, etc. Purposeful, personal, reflective, slow-down moments that will allow you to make the biggest impact of all – on yourself. You haven't done this in a while, have you? You have been so focused on your business, on employees, clients, competitors, and others, that you have forgotten the highest return investment you can make - in you.

The next ripple is that of your family, your friends, and the relationships that you may want to strengthen and build. Perhaps it is spending more time with your spouse, seeing your kids and grandkids, joining a golf league, or other social activities that will satisfy your need for connection and gently populate your social schedule. You still largely create and manage your own calendar; your days are filled with choices. You will grow and become more enjoyable to be around - trust this. A friendly, sociable, relaxed, wise person will attract like-minded and like-hearted people. Build your future from the inside out.

The last, and perhaps most broad and far-reaching ripple, is choosing acts of service following your career. Imagine joining boards, advising and supporting non-profits, and engaging civically, perhaps in local or regional public service. Does this speak to you? For folks who find themselves a bit restless and not yet ready to let go of a fast-paced, external-facing life, this third ring of service and giving back may be incredibly fulfilling, and necessary.

Now, that is not to say that you can't maintain balance across all three. Some people go all in on one and forget the others. Your choice now is yours and yours alone. The balance you seek and ultimately strike can and should be carefully thought out. The people you connect with and impact, whether they are family, friends, or the public – deserve a rested, reflective, whole version of you. And after years, decades in some instances, this version is finally possible. Don't they deserve it? Don't you?

The end is the beginning

We have said this multiple times throughout the book, and this time, we surely mean it - you have come to the end of this chapter, and this book. The end of this book may mark the official, first act of your succession journey. In some ways, the genie is out of the bottle. Can you now look at succession planning the same? Do you think you can make it on your own, without a plan, advisors, or a clear framework through which you will make personal, business, and life decisions? Can you fend off a choppy exit and make your way, solo, through the tumultuous chapters of succession execution, a sale, or an exit?

Chances are you have earmarked pages or written notes to yourself. Maybe you have a list. The good news is that this book is all about how to approach your succession journey, not a prescriptive how-to manual. Leading, and leaving, is an art, not a science. There are tried and tested methods of business management, but ultimately, it comes down to you, the person you have been, and the person you will be.

Who will you be moving forward? Who is counting on you now? What will your legacy be?

Consider the fresh new chapter you are going to write in your life through business succession – the journey to, through, and after. What support do you need? What advice and perspective will help you make the very best decisions for the people you care about the most?

Small, deliberate actions are laid out in this book. Frameworks, vignettes, and lessons can all be used to glean insight into how you will authentically author one of the most important chapters of your life. Apply them. Assemble help. Ask an advisor for support and to hold you accountable towards the finish line. Because, as we know, this is just the beginning of the rest of your life.

This moment is yours. The next steps are waiting for you. Take them, and do not look back.

A FINAL NOTE

As business owners and leaders, it is incredibly difficult to move on from the identity we have forged for ourselves. If you are like me, you likely enjoy the freedom, pressure, and reward of working for yourself, and being responsible for the direction, and success, of an organization.

Which is why it is nearly impossible to imagine giving up the feeling you get when times are good, and even when times are tough. The pressure of figuring it all out. The high of winning.

In watching clients, family, and even reflecting on my own experience, I continue to land in the same place. The music in fact does have to stop. The page does have to turn. At some point we, as founders, have to allow for someone else to carry the torch. We fight this truth as it nears. We stand in our own way and tell ourselves that we still have a few, good years left.

I cannot stress how important it is to accept the realization that if you outstay your tenure as an owner and leader, your business will eventually decline. Accepting the truths that are laid out in this book, and in your own life, is the key to unlocking your future, and to moving forward in your life. It is the key for your business, for your people, and for your family as well.

Reflect on these chapters. Reflect on the thoughts you are having about your past, your present, and your future. And if you find yourself continuing to ponder the steps needed, and wonder about the journey ahead, please do not hesitate to reach out. I welcome a call.

Sincerely, Alex Teece

www.ingramcontent.com/pod-product-compliance
Lightning Source LLC
Chambersburg PA
CBHW070943210326
41520CB00021B/7031